How to sell your Handmade Jewellery

Brenda Hunt

Marketing for Small Business Series

Marketing for Small Businesses

Copyright © Brenda Hunt 2012

All rights reserved world wide
No part of 'How to sell your handmade jewellery' may be reproduced or stored by any means without the express permission of Brenda Hunt

Whilst reasonable care is taken to ensure the accuracy of the information in this publication, no responsibility can be accepted for the consequences of any actions based on any opinions, information or advice found in the publication.

Any Business information contained in this publication should not be taken as a substitute for professional advice. It is your own responsibility to comply with all legal, accounting and tax regulations. Please seek advice from your legal and accounting advisors. The author and publisher of this book used their best efforts in producing this book and disclaim liability arising directly or indirectly from the use of the information in this book.

ISBN-13: 978-1480235700
ISBN-10: 1480235709

Introduction	6
What is Marketing and Why is it important?	8
Why should you care about marketing?	8
What is marketing?	8
Market research	10
Market research, part two	13
Craft shops and events	14
Who is your customer	17
Where will you sell?	20
Craft fairs.	21
School or church fairs	23
County shows	24
Christmas markets	25
Wedding fairs.	26
House parties	30
Markets	33
Talks to social and church groups	35
Demonstrations	38
Be prepared to expand	38
What's your style?	40
Focus your attention	40
Who is your target customer	43
Creating your brand	43

- Designing your logo — 44
- Unique Selling Point — 46

Presenting Yourself — 48
- Setting out your stall — 48
- The cover. — 48
- Height — 50
- Display stands — 51
- Lighting — 53
- Exhibition Banners — 54
- The rest of your equipment bag — 55

Packaging your product — 57
- Creating an image — 57
- Plastic or card tab tops — 59
- Organza bags and velvet pouches — 59
- Jewellery boxes. — 60
- Packaging the packaging — 62

Pricing your jewellery — 64
- Work out the cost of each piece — 65
- Your wholesale price — 68
- Setting the price of your product — 68

How to Promote yourself — 72
- Price promotions — 72
- Bundled discounts — 73

Time specific discounts.	74
Free gifts	74
Sale time	75
Product promotion.	76
Talking about your jewellery.	77
Demonstrating your craft.	79
Seasonal promotions	80
The Christmas season	81
Growing your business.	86
Where will you go from here	86
Selling online.	87
The future	89
A final word	90
The Business of Business	90
Find some expert advice	90

Introduction

Everyone loves jewellery.

You only need to see how many places sell jewellery to decide that this is true. And it's not anything new. People have loved jewellery throughout history, whether it was protective amulets, Royal regalia, a decoration for the wealthy and powerful, an expression of love or a treat to yourself. Today, jewellery is everywhere, in every style and at every price range and available to all.

Making your own jewellery takes this love of beautiful things a step further. You can create exactly what you want, choosing your colours, your style and the length that suits you, rather than having to choose from the selection offered to you. It opens up a whole new world of self-expression.

And now you have taken the decision that you are ready to offer your beautiful handmade creations to the rest of the world.

There are a number of ways of presenting your jewellery to the public and this book is aimed at helping you to sell it face to face, directly to your customers rather than through shops or craft outlets or online.

What will make your jewellery stand out from the crowd? And one thing is certain, you will find a crowd of other jewellery stalls at almost every event you attend, but you shouldn't let that put you off. This book will show you how to stand out from that crowd, how to succeed not only in-spite of the competition - but because of it!

When you market your jewellery properly, the very fact that you are surrounded by others who don't, will make your jewellery look better.

So, this book will guide you through the whole process. How to create your style, how to promote your business, how to layout your shopfront. How to decide on packaging and presentation.

It will also give you some ideas about where you can set up your shopfront. Craft fairs are the obvious first step, but you might choose to do wedding fairs, markets, country fairs, or party plan. You might even decide to do all of them!

Whether your aim is to simply pay for your jewellery addiction, make some extra money for holidays or take the plunge and start your own business empire, this book will help you plan and design and make the most of your exciting new venture.

What is Marketing and Why is it important?

Why should you care about marketing?

Why am I starting with marketing? It's because marketing is at the heart of any successful professional venture. In fact, this whole book is really about marketing and how you can use marketing to create your new business and to grow to whichever level of business you want.

Some people will be happy to keep their jewellery business small, a home business that is focused on one person. Some will expand it to a family business selling on-line and through some craft shops as well as face to face, and others will want to create a brand that will be found in stores across the country.

But in this book we are focusing on the early stages of your new business and how to make the best of your opportunities when selling direct to your customer face-to-face.

What is marketing?

Many small businesses make the mistake of thinking that the whole concept of marketing is only something for big business.

That it's the world of the Marketing Director, huge budgets, huge departments, specialist agencies and the multi-national companies.

But at its heart, marketing is basic common sense.

Know what your customer wants - and supply it.

In fact, it's such basic common sense that some huge multi-national companies, with their huge marketing budgets and high powered marketing departments, completely lose sight of it, and then they lose sight of their customers as they leave in droves and go somewhere else that does still supply what they want.

Think of the mess some of the big high street names get themselves into when they decided that they know better than their customers. They start losing their customers - which for any company, means losing your business - and it can take them years and a huge amount of work to get them back.

Another misconception is that Sales and Marketing are the same thing - but they're not.

A Sales Campaign - selling your idea to the public and persuading them that they can't live without your product, can be a very expensive process. TV adverts, billboards, newspaper & magazine advertising are well out of reach for a small business. The world of the Internet and social media has opened it up if you are savvy with the technology, but it still doesn't get you the huge coverage and it still isn't the same as marketing. Companies can and have, spent huge amounts of money on trying to sell a product but failed at the end of the day because they're failed on the basic principle of marketing - they're trying to sell something that people don't want!

So, although some things may be out of the

reach of the small business, really good marketing is something that the smallest of start up business can - indeed have to be - really good at.

After all, if you can't afford an expensive TV advertising campaign you'd better make sure that you're supplying exactly what your customer is looking for!

Market research

Every successful business knows who their target audience is. Look around at shops, magazines, fashion companies, car companies, holiday companies and of course jewellery companies.

Take one area of business and really look at them in detail rather than just at the ones that you normally buy from.

For instance spend a day at your nearest large shopping centre and study the stores that sell clothes - you need to visit a large shopping centre so that you have a full range of outlets to study.

You may never have really thought about it, but you'll know which ones attract you personally and which ones you'd never think of shopping in. But what is it about the brands and their shops that give you these signals?

This time really look at all of them, really study them.

Who do they target?
What age range?
What style?
What budget?

Decide what type of people would shop in that store.

What age, what life style, what career?

Where would they go for the evening? What type of holiday would they take? What type of car would they buy? And how can you tell that?

For this process, don't worry about being judgmental - you are trying to judge, you're learning how to judge what type of customer is going to want your jewellery!

Apart from the prices - which might not always be obvious straight away (in-fact the presence or absence of obvious prices can tell you something as well) - how can you tell the difference between the budget shop and the expensive?

What is the difference in the shopping experience between the designer boutique and the outlet that sells quality classic pieces?

Look at the decor of the shops, the colours, the style of their furnishings, the way they use the space.

How do they display their stock? Is every inch of space used or do they display a smaller number of pieces, giving each individual outfit space to be seen? Do they sell a jacket or do they sell the whole outfit as a 'look'.

How do they package their product? You don't actually have to purchase anything, although that can be fun and is certainly a way of finding out how they treat their customers, how they make you feel about your purchase and the whole experience of dealing with the company.

But if you decide that the process of market research doesn't stretch to a £350 Mulberry purse (sad but true!) just find a coffee shop or seat close to the shop and watch customers come and go. Is their purchase just stuffed into a plastic bag or is it carefully wrapped in tissue paper and gently placed in a beautiful, branded bag with ribbon handles? Think of what you would prefer as a customer.

Times are tough at the moment and it seems that they are going to stay that way for a while yet, so parting with money should be a pleasure. The experience should be fun, enjoyable and memorable for the right reasons. After all, when you buy new clothes, chocolates, cosmetics or a piece of jewellery, it's a treat, no matter how much or little you're parting with, so it should feel like you're getting a treat rather than feeling the same as when you're just buying a tin of beans.

You can see the same range of experiences in almost any market.

A lipstick can be picked up in the supermarket with the weekly shop or it can be a luxurious treat in a beautiful gold case, picked out for you by someone elegant who takes the time to find the right shade for you and then packs it in a lovely gift bag with some free samples of other items in the range.

You might say that a lipstick is a lipstick, but in times of austerity sales of luxury lipsticks go up. Women might not be able to afford the Dior outfit or the Chanel handbag, but they can afford the lipstick or the eye shadow.

Market research, part two

Now that you've looked at how people shop and more importantly, how companies sell to them, you need to bring your market research closer to home.

Why you're still in the shopping centre, focus your attention on jewellery shops, jewellery departments in the big stores and the barrows in the shopping malls.

Can you tell what their target audience is? How do they create an image?

Remember, they are the professionals at this and they have spent a great deal of time and money to create the look that they want, the look that will attract the target audience that they want and then get them to part with their money. Learn from their experience!

Although you won't be creating a complete jewellery store or department, there will still be signals that you can take away with you and learn from.

What sort of colours have they used in their displays? Is it displayed on jewellery stands as individual pieces, or are they on tags and all hung together on a wire spinner? Is the display crowded like an Aladdin's cave or does each individual piece of jewellery have its own space, even its own display stand?

How do they package the jewellery? How do they physically price it? Is it a price sticker on the tag, does a general price cover every piece on the display or are they priced individually, with neat little stands? Of course if you're looking at a very exclusive jewellery store, they probably are not priced at all, on the basis that if you have to ask the price you can't afford it! You probably don't want to copy that pattern, you might want to, but that would take a lot of building up to!

What signals tell you the price range without even looking at the price?

Once you've actually looked at how things are sold and started to recognise what the subtle signals are in the selling process, you can begin to decide what signals you want to give to your potential customers and how you will go about that.

Craft shops and events

If you're interested in creating your own handcrafted creations, you've almost certainly been visiting craft fairs, craft shops and gift shops for many years, but you probably haven't looked critically at them.

You now want to start visiting them and looking with a more detailed eye. After all, you are about to become part of this world. Although you're looking at the overall image you are specifically looking at how they sell jewellery.

What does the jewellery look like, what image does it create? Without looking at the prices, what price range would you judge that it falls into and who is it aimed at?

What signals make you think that?

When you did look at the prices, are they in the range that you expected or are they cheaper or more expensive than you thought they would be. What is giving you these signals?

Is the jewellery that's displayed giving you the image of pocket money pieces, but is actually priced as exclusive fine jewellery? Or are you looking at beautiful pieces of jewellery that you think will be in a higher price range, actually being sold at costume jewellery prices?

Either of these extremes will actually lose you potential customers.

I vividly remember visiting an art market in America over 20 years ago. There were many crafters with permanent stalls selling a wide range of items from T shirts and handwoven shawls to novelty number plates and shell ornaments, and I visited it a number of times during the holiday. One of the stallholders was selling beautiful handmade silver jewellery, beautifully laid out and none of it priced. The designs were very unusual, the display was very clean and uncluttered and whereas many of the other stalls were frequently crowded with potential customers, this one was not. During many visits, I looked at the jewellery and admired it, but I didn't actually go into the store area, because the jewellery looked as if it was above my price bracket. Towards the end of the holiday, I decided I had to at least have a closer look at it, I never have been able to resist jewellery! To my absolute amazement it was actually very reasonably priced, costing far less than many of the other tourist items and gifts that were being sold in the rest of the art market. Luckily, I hadn't bought all of the presents I wanted to bring home. So I was able to purchase some of these unique works of art for friends as well as myself. The problem is, if I had only made one visit to this art market, I wouldn't have purchased anything at all from this wonderful jewellery store, because the signals it was giving off were totally wrong.

So when you visit craft fairs, or when you're selling at craft fairs, take a look around at other stalls and see how they display their jewellery and what signals, they are giving the potential customer.

Now that you've learned how to really look, you will be able to pick up on the displays that work and the ones that don't.

Which ones are attracting people and which ones do people pass by without looking. It isn't always to do with the quality of the jewellery. Some people selling beautifully made jewellery are just not attracting people's attention.

You can continue to learn and fine tune your own shopfront as you do more events. You will learn over time what did work, and even more importantly, what didn't work.

Once you start fine tuning the process, you will discover that different venues require you to adapt your display. A part of the stall that you use to catch people's attention may have to be at the left end of the table in some venues and at the right end in others, depending on which way the traffic moves around the room. I have been known to re-organise an entire 12 foot display halfway through a fair!

Who is your customer

Now that you have done some serious market research, you can begin to decide who your jewellery is aimed at.

No matter how tempting it might seem, you cannot be all things to all people, you have to choose who your target audience is.

Where do you want to place yourself in what is after all a very crowded market?

You have to take a number of things into account.

Where will you be selling?

Who will your customer be?

Do you want to sell fashion jewellery or designer fine jewellery?

What style of jewellery do you make or want to make - boho or pearls? Stretch bracelets or gemstone pendants?

You can either decide where you are going to sell and what type of customer you will have and what they will want, and set yourself up to design for that market.

Or you can decide what type of jewellery you make or want to make and find an outlet that will attract the type of customer for your style and price range.

The problem is that it's not always easy - or possible - to find exactly the outlet you want - either in the area that you are based or at the rent that you can afford to pay - especially at first.

There's not much point deciding that you want to sell high end designer jewellery at upwards of £100 a piece if you can't find a place to sell it from or Gothic chic in a quiet area that doesn't get a regular supply of Goths to adore your masterpieces.

The beauty about running a small business is that you can be adaptable. In fact that's one of your greatest strengths. You don't have to go through planning meetings, committees, getting approval and deciding on budgets, arranging purchasing, suppliers and mountains of other planning. You can get an idea, decide what you need to do and go and do it! See a trend and be selling it within weeks, sometimes within days if you have the parts. You can constantly adapt and change to a changing market.

So, probably the best way of deciding on your style is a mixture of what you like making and what price range you think will sell.

Don't be scared to be different. You don't simply want to churn out what everybody else is selling, or copy what you think is a popular style in the local supermarket. Put some of your own character into your jewellery is what will help you create your own distinct style. Whether that is the type of colours that you use, the fact that you make your own paper or clay beads, or that you like making macramé jewellery. Whoever your customer is, one of the real delights of buying handmade jewellery directly from the designer is the fact that you are buying something that you can't get in the local shops, and that you won't see everybody else wearing.

Where will you sell?

This book is mainly aimed at the process of selling face-to-face, directly to your customer.

Of course there are other ways of selling your hamdmade designs nowadays. People often think of selling online first, through etsy, eBay, Amazon or your own website. Or you could decide to sell through craft and gift shops or wholesale to other outlets. And that's fine, but there's still plenty of chances to sell directly to your customers.

- Craft fairs
- School or church fairs
- County shows
- Christmas markets
- Wedding fairs.
- House parties
- Markets
- Talks to WI or other groups
- Demonstrations

You may decide to use some or all of these methods to sell your jewellery direct to the customer, but if you're looking at this list for the first time, how do the different events differ?

Although you can often make bookings at quite short notice, especially if for smaller events that might be planned close to the date or if there have been cancellations at some of the more established events, many booking are made about a year in advance.

You should be prepared to start planning your annual calendar in January to make sure that you are at the most successful events.

Craft fairs.

This is probably the section you will think of first when you decide to sell your handmade jewellery direct to the customer face-to-face.

You've probably visited quite a number of craft fairs over the years, but once you step onto the other side of the counter there is actually quite a lot to know about craft fairs.

There's a huge variety in the type of event, the size of event, how much rent you will have to pay, how many days you will have to commit and what is expected from you as a craftsperson.

At one end of the scale, you will find small local events, where you can simply book a six-foot table and pay about £20-£30 for the day. Tables are normally supplied, although for some fairs you do have to supply your own, in which case a wallpaper pasting table is normally first choice but you'll probably move on to a more sturdy version after you've completed a few fairs.

As a general guide, most of these fairs start at about 10am and close at about 4pm with the venue being open from about 8am to 5pm to allow you time to set up and then clear away again afterwards.

The organisers for most of these smaller events will expect you to be on time, stay to the end of the fair, pay your table rent and sell only your own hand made goods. Many of them will also require you to have public and product liability insurance.

Many of these organisers run fairs throughout the year, either a regular event at a specific venue or a programme of events at different venues that repeats throughout the year. As you book more fairs you will get to know more crafts people and they tend to be very generous with their knowledge and will let you know who else to contact about different events.

Customers are often very loyal to a series of events and they will follow them to different venues or to the same venue year after year, so you automatically have a very good opportunity of building up a regular following. If you develop a distinctive style, people will collect your jewellery and comeback season after season looking for your latest designs, which of course is a very good reason to keep your designs fresh.

Other organisers will arrange larger events at a specific venue, often their own, once or twice a year. These can be at garden centres, hotels and shopping centres, or even in town centres. They will normally be two or three day events and will quite often cost £150 a day or more plus VAT. You will definitely require public and product liability insurance before you're allowed to book and any electrical equipment you use will have to have a PAT certificate (portable appliance testing).

Some of these events will be craft and gift fairs which can have pros and cons. It means that you can sell items you have bought in, but it also means that your beautiful handmade pieces will be competing directly against mass-market jewellery from China.

A larger event will attract more people, which means more potential customers. As well as being prepared to speculate more time and money you will also have to have more stock, so that you can make the most of the larger number of people passing your stall.

School or church fairs

School and church fairs are quite often much shorter events, possibly only two or three hours during the afternoon or in the evening. They can also be midweek, whereas most craft fairs are focused on the weekend. This means that they are easy to fit in around your main schedule. You can quite often leave a large event at about 4pm on Saturday, go and do a small school fair in the evening, and be back at the large event on Sunday morning. Try not to do this too often as it can be very tiring!

Although they are smaller events, and they will cost you less rent, they are often quite well attended by people who have every intention of purchasing. Small fairs tend to happen at certain times of the year, around Easter, in the summer and for Christmas. Once you are on an organisers list, you will tend to become a regular. doing the same fairs year after year, hopefully attracting a loyal following. Many charity events also fall into the same pattern.

County shows

County shows, town fairs or big events such as air shows and flower festivals often have a craft marquee as part of the show.

The way this is organised can vary enormously on the type of show. For instance, a local county show can be organised by a committee of local people while some of the large flower festivals are organised by the Royal Horticultural Society will normally have their craft marquee organised by one of the Craft Guilds and Associations. For the first type of show, you simply apply as you would with any other event, but for the second you need to be a member of the relevant Crafts Guild.

Most of these shows are held in marquees, hopefully, but not necessarily in good weather, so you should be prepared for the British summer! In fact being prepared is a vital part of making a success of this type of show. Check on the weather forecast and dress for the event, spending an extended time in a marquee can be either very cold or very hot - rarely in the middle. So either have warm clothes and waterproof shoes or have a fan! You also have to take into account that they can be cancelled if the weather is really bad. Some of our recent wet summers have caused havoc with the events calendar and this can have a disastrous affect of your cash flow if you have been depending on the income from a number of big events.

Most of the shows will be at least two days, many of them can last more and some up to a full week, so you need to make sure that you have plenty of stock.

The rent for this type of show can also vary enormously depending on whether it is a local event or a large national event. Some organisers would require you to sign quite long contracts and it is worth reading these to make sure that you know what you are committing yourself to. One thing to look out for is the clause on cancellation. There are organisers, who will not refund your money even if they cancel the event which could result in you losing a large upfront investment, possibly the cost of accommodation and of course the loss of the opportunity to sell altogether for that weekend. These larger events are a significant investment in time and money, and only you will be able to decide whether it suits you or not, and at what stage in your business it might suit you.

When they work, large shows can bring in large amounts of money and are very worthwhile doing, but it's probably not a good idea to rely on them totally at first.

Christmas markets

Christmas markets are quite obviously held at Christmas!

They've become very popular in recent years, and they tend to be organised by towns and cities to be held as part of the general Christmas festivities.

Although they do vary from town to town, many of them last a number of weeks and take the form of stalls in the town centre. Sometimes they are the standard market stalls under canvas while some towns set individual wooden huts and others set aside a section of the indoor market or an indoor shopping centre.

Again, if they are outside you have to be prepared for the weather if you decide to do this type of event. Being outside in the winter in Britain can certainly be cold! You will also have to set up and dismantle your stall each day as obviously you cannot leave anything open overnight in the middle of the town centre.

If you are concentrating on Christmas, make sure that you make it easy for the customer to see your jewellery as a Christmas present. Again learn from the stores, in a Christmas market you are competing directly with them.

Wedding fairs.

Wedding fairs are very specific events.

Many jewellers specialise in creating wedding jewellery, so that they not only make pendants, necklaces, earrings and bracelets, but they also design tiaras, hair combs, fascinators and even cufflinks and tiepins.

Special orders and bespoke designs are an important part of being a wedding jeweller. In a bridal store the bride has to choose from what is available. When she comes to you, she can have a design created specifically for her, including the colours that she wants for her wedding.

This can be a very interesting and lucrative area

to specialise in.

Wedding fairs are very often held at wedding venues such as hotels and civic centres. You will find that there is quite a difference in the cost of a wedding fair as opposed to a craft fair. A six-foot table at a craft fair could cost £50, while the same six-foot table in the same room at a wedding fair could cost £150.

You will also need to think specifically about how you design your table for a wedding fair. The event itself is different. Other stallholders will not be other crafters, they will be professional photographers, wedding dress shops, printers who specialise in wedding stationery, cake designers, suppliers of wedding cars, event organisers, make-up artists and hairdressers.

Many of them will have professional display stands and equipment that they bring from their shops. This doesn't mean that you have to suddenly invest thousands of pounds in professional shopfitting equipment, but it does mean that you have to look very professional.

If you use white cloths make sure that they are a nice heavy quality and of course are spotlessly clean. Although many people choose white, you might decide to stand out from the crowd by using a colour. It's entirely your choice and I always feel that beautiful white pearl jewellery shows up better on something rich like burgundy!

Although it is very nice if you can make any sales at the event, doing a wedding fair is mainly about future sales and orders. So it is vital that you have some information that the potential bride can take away with her.

As I mentioned, most of your fellow exhibitors will be wedding professionals. This can have its drawbacks for them, which is potential for you.

Many of them will be manned (or womaned!) by people who work for the company and a lot of them will simply sit behind their stands expecting potential clients to pick up their leaflets. At the other extreme, others will be at the side of their stand shoving their leaflets into any hand that passes, whether the person shows any interest or not.

You will have a chance to be different. Smile at people, engage with them, talk to them. Exhibiting at the wedding fair is all about making connections with people so that they will remember you and so that you will have the opportunity to contact them.

Gathering a list of contacts is vital, because very often, a bride and groom will be looking for ideas for the wedding that can be up to 2 years in the future. So you need to be able to keep in contact with them. Collect names and addresses and e-mail addresses, and the date of their wedding so that you can target your marketing to suit their timescale.

Don't be afraid of having slightly quirky designs. After all, a bride who simply wants white pearls and silver crystals can buy her jewellery from hundreds of different places. The bride who wants something different is much more likely to notice you if you don't just display what is expected traditionally.

As with all parts of your handmade jewellery business, you can't possibly be all things to all people. Even if you could produce every style of jewellery you can't produce enough of it to sell to everybody. So you may as well specialise in a niche that you enjoy and become a big player in a small niche. Some of my most successful wedding designs have featured rich colours such as Amethyst, deep red Garnets or rich and vibrant orange carnelian. While not every bride wants to stick to the traditional pale whites and ivories, it's not always easy to find a bridal tiara that features rich purple Amethyst.

One of your main selling points is that you are the creator of unique handmade jewellery, rather than a seller of mass produced jewellery. So have a selection of your beads and crystals with you at the event. This means that you will be able to show the bride the various colours she could choose from. You could even make a small hair clip for her using these colours and attach it to your business card as a gift. Actually making jewellery at your stand will always attract attention. The ideal situation is being able to get the bride to place their order for this bespoke handcrafted jewellery, choosing the designs and particularly the colours so that she will have her own unique wedding designs

House parties

Selling by party plan at house parties can be a very successful way of selling your handmade jewellery.

Some of the more traditional party plan has gone out of fashion, after all there is only so much Tupperware that you really want! But that doesn't mean that the idea of party plan is out of date, far from it, it just means that people are looking for more unusual reasons to have a party.

Unique handmade pieces of jewellery are ideal for this. Most women love jewellery, jewellery is a very easy present to give to others and you can have enough of a price range to make it comfortable for everybody at the party. Because although some people can quite comfortably afford to spend £70 or £80, in these more economically challenging times there are many others who would be relieved to be able to just spend £5 or £10 without embarrassment.

Once you have started doing house parties, they do have a tendency to feed of themselves, in fact that's the whole idea of a successful party plan business. Someone, preferably two people at the party will book parties of their own and invite different selections of people, which will lead on again to more bookings and more new customers.

Obviously the best way to start is if you can persuade some of your friends to hold a party for you. But you can also arrange to work with someone who already does party plan with a different product and is willing to let you join them.

You should also advertise the fact that you do parties at every other event that you attend.

There are a few main things you need to do, to create a successful party plan business.

Make it easy for the host to have a party.

Create invitations or leaflets that they can hand out to their friends. People need to know what to expect to see for sale at the party and how much they expect the items to cost, so that they have an idea of the price ranges. They also need to know when and where it is. It's a good idea to put some photos of your jewellery onto the invitation and if you have a website put the address on so that they can go and have a look at the type of handmade jewellery you have for sale. And do emphasise that it is handmade, by you rather than just mass produced and available at the market.

Make it worthwhile for the host to have a party.

She will be going to quite a lot of trouble and some expense, providing wine and nibbles at least for her guests, as well as putting the time in to arrange the party. So it has to be worth her while. You can decide on the exact style of your incentive, but generally it will be something like a percentage of the value of your total sales in the evening to be spent on her own order. The percentage is up to you, but is normally somewhere between 10% and 20%. You could also decide to give a bonus for each person that books a further party, or a special offer only available to the organiser on the evening. The more creative you can be, the more successful you should be in booking future parties. After all, people are more likely to book a party of their own if they feel it's going to be worthwhile to them.

Make it easy to set up your party.

For both your sake and your host's sake, you don't want to spend two hours setting up your display! Design an easy and time efficient way of carrying and setting out your range. You have a limited amount of time and space when doing a house party, so don't try to take every design you've ever made. Decide from your experience, what your bestsellers are and make sure that you have them together with enough variety for people to have a choice, but not so much that it overwhelms them.

Make it interesting for the host and her guests.

Don't just put your jewellery out and expect it to sell itself. Don't just stand in a corner like a wallflower. Give a short talk that explains something about your jewellery, what makes it special, what makes it different, do you use genuine gemstones and precious metals. Or do you make your own beads. Give them an idea of the price range, show how you can put a set of jewellery together. Talk about how you can design special pieces for them. How bracelets can be made at a size to suit, because each one is handmade. Many women have a problem with bracelets, because they do tend to come in one size fits all, which means that women with a very slender wrist or a heavy wrist often can't find bracelets that will fit.

Make it easy for the guests to make a purchase.

Most party plan businesses rely on people placing an order and receiving it at a later date. Personally I always have my selection of my handmade jewellery for them to take away on the night. Although there are some times when a number of people want the same design, this is quite unusual, after all the beauty of handmade jewellery is that it is different from everyone else. If it does happen, then I will take the order and post the piece out to them directly rather than expecting the host of the party to do the deliveries for me.

Finally make it easy and worthwhile for the guests to book a party of their own. The life blood of a party plan business is to continually book new parties. If you book one party from each party that you do, your business will stay level. If you book two parties from each party you do your business will grow. But if you don't book any parties, your business will die.

Markets

Many towns hold regular markets. Some of these are general markets, some of them are farmers markets, and some of them are craft markets. Which type you might decide to take a stall at is entirely up to you. Different markets suit different crafters, but there are some general rules that apply to any of them.

Most market organisers will supply the stalls, which are normally a metal framework covered by a (mostly) waterproof canvass. They will also normally supply the table top for you to set your product out on. You will have to supply your own covers, and of course you won't have electricity in most cases.

Markets take place on every day of the week. Some towns have a weekly market, whereas others are held on every day of the week. Many market traders have a weekly route around their local towns, setting up shop every morning in the next town. As a crafter it is highly unlikely that you will follow that pattern as you need time to create your product, so you would probably only do two or maybe three regular days a week.

Some of the indoor markets have space allocated for a specialist Craft fair that they hold once a month. Although these are held in markets, they do follow more the pattern of the craft fair. You will have a 6 foot table as your stall and you probably will have an electrical supply.

Markets whether indoor or outside, are very open areas, with the public milling around, rather than people who have chosen to come into a craft fair. This means that you can have a much wider range of potential customers, but it also means that you have to be more aware of the risk of shoplifters. Make sure that any expensive pieces of jewellery are out of the way of sticky fingers and take care of your cash.

If you are planning on doing many markets, it is worth joining the National Market Traders Federation, membership of which gives you public and product liability insurance, as well as many other benefits.

Talks to social and church groups

There are many groups who are constantly looking for people to give talks at their monthly meetings.

Obviously, many of the people who will give talks will require some payment to cover their costs.

If you are able to take a selection of your products with you that are available for their members to purchase, then you can offer to give the talk without charge. You are taking the risk that you will give the talk and not take any money, but personally, I have never had this happen. In fact, many of these events can be extremely lucrative.

I always give a gift to the organisation that they can use as a raffle prize, sometimes on the night, sometimes with a raffle to be held at a later date, it's their choice. As a jewellery maker, you can give a gift that is worth a lot more than it costs you to produce.

Many members of such groups are members of more than one, so as always, do make sure that everyone has your contact details. As with party plan, you will find that you make bookings from bookings.

Again, as with party plan, make it easy to set up your display.

For both your sake and the groups sake, you don't want to spend two hours setting up your stand! They will often only have access to the hall about half an hour before the start of their meeting. Normally, they will deal with group business, such as reading the minutes, first and then hand the rest of the meeting over to you. You will have to be able to set up your display quickly and quietly. You will also need to be able to pack it away quickly once the meeting is over.

Design an easy and time efficient way of carrying and setting out your range, don't try to take every design you've ever made. You will also have to be flexible about how you set out your display. As you want to know beforehand what type of tables, they will supply.

Decide from your experience what your bestsellers are and make sure that you have them, together with enough variety for people to have a choice, but not so much that it overwhelms them. You'll find over time that your bestsellers vary from venue to venue and event type to event type. Keep a record of what you sell so that you can see any patterns that emerge.

Make it interesting for the group, you are there to give a talk after all. Don't just put your jewellery out and expect it to sell itself, selling anything is supposed to be a bonus at this type of event. Give a short talk that explains something about your jewellery, what makes it special, what makes it different, do you use genuine gemstones and precious metals or do you make your own beads.

For this type of talk, you can get more personal, because they are not just interested in buying the jewellery, they are interested in what drew you into making jewellery. How did you learn? How long have you been making jewellery? Where do you get your design inspiration? What made you decide to set up business?

Give them an idea of the price range, show how you can put a set of jewellery together. Talk about how you can design special pieces for them. How bracelets can be made at a size to suit, because each one is handmade. Many women have a problem with bracelets, because they do tend to come in one size fits all, which means that women with a very slender wrist or a heavy wrist often can't find bracelets that will fit.

Once you have finished your talk, which you should keep to about 20 to 30 minutes, be prepared for a rush! This is not a leisurely day long craft fair, everybody wants to be served within about 15 minutes before they rush off to get a bus, meet someone who's giving them a lift, or just get home!

These talks can take place during the day or in the evenings and at any time of the week, depending on what type of group you are talking to. So you can fit quite a number into your calendar. They are often booked over a year in advance as the social secretary arranges the plan for the year.

Demonstrations

Demonstrations are a great way of selling. It shows people that you do actually know what you're doing. They love seeing how something is made, that it is actually a handcrafted piece of jewellery created in front of them. If you can set aside some space to demonstrate you will normally be able to gather a crowd to your stall. Some organisers will give you extra space if you are willing to demonstrate, because they know that this is a draw for the public.

There are also times when you will be asked to simply go and demonstrate your craft. This can be in a craft store, where they want to sell the beads. It can be at a school or youth club, where they would like you to teach others how to make jewellery.

One of the benefits of this is that it creates an image for you as an expert in your field. And as well as leading to work demonstrating or teaching it can also lead to sales and special orders for your jewellery.

Be prepared to expand

So as you can see, there are many different ways of reaching out to your customer in face-to-face situations.

Most people do start out with local craft fairs, but as you begin to do these craft shows, you will find that other opportunities open up to you and you should always make sure that you are prepared for the opportunity. Many organisers arranging new events, or looking for new stallholders for their well-established events, will visit other craft fairs looking for fresh ideas and new designers.

Other organisers looking for speakers for their regular meetings or craftspeople who are willing to come to their workplaces, callcentres or nursing homes and set up stall for a few hours will visit craft fairs to look for suitable ideas.

Some of these organisers will actually stop to talk to you, but others prefer to simply pick up your business card or leaflet and call you at a later date. So obviously it is very important to have a business card or leaflet on your stall.

If you do a number of events, prepare a leaflet that lists them all so that people can follow you around. Regular customers are very valuable and they will also recommend you to their friends.

Include your contact details on this leaflet, your business name, your phone number, your e-mail address and website but be very careful about putting your geographical address. If you work from home, you are effectively giving people a list of dates when your home will be empty!

If you would like to do party plan or talks, add this to your leaflet. You can also produce a more detailed leaflet about your party plan arrangements, which you can hand out to people if they ask about it.

What's your style?

You probably haven't thought about it before, you just make jewellery for your own pleasure probably as gifts for friends and family, maybe even for orders from friends and work colleagues. Most small jewellery businesses start off like this, almost by accident.

But all along you will have been developing a style, even if it's not well-defined yet.

Now is the time to think about it. When you decide to take the step to selling your jewellery, which you have or are about to if you're reading this book, you need to start developing a style of your own.

No business, no matter how large it is, can be all things to all people. And when you're a small business that is even more true. So rather than trying to do everything, concentrate on one thing and do it really well.

Focus your attention

There are many interpretations of style. I don't mean that you should only make Amethyst jewellery, or one design of gemstone earrings, although that could work. After all, what comes to mind when you think of the brand Pandora? Bracelets and charms, even though they do make other styles of jewellery. That could seem rather limited, but Pandora doesn't seem to have been at all limited by it.

You can find other examples of big brands, some of which specialise in designs that are quite simple. Gemstone bead stretch bracelets or bead necklaces, but that hasn't stopped them becoming large, well-known brands.

So, look at the jewellery you make and decide what the main elements are.

Do you work with precious metals, copper, sterling silver or gold vermile and 9ct gold. Or do you work with silverplated and goldplated parts? Maybe your main designs are done with bead stringing or macramé or wire work.

Do you work with gemstones, if so are they beads, cabochon or faceted gemstones? How do you use them, do you string them or set cabochons into precious metal cast settings.

Do you work with acrylic beads, glass, exclusive Murano glass, wooden or clay beads? Or are your designs quirky, based on old buttons or other vintage pieces? Do you make your own glass pendants or polymer clay beads?

Do you make dainty pendants or chunky bead necklaces. Do you work with subtle colours or a riot of brights or perhaps you prefer a palette of blacks!

Once you start to think about it, you'll find that you do actually have a style of your own, a style that you can develop and become known for.

When you've decided on your main style and what you feel you want to concentrate on, you can begin to make decisions about what you think your jewellery design and image should be.

At this stage it's probably worth discarding some of the designs that really don't fit into your new design style.

As we decided earlier, you can't be all things to all people, so now is the time to think about who your target customer is.

If your range is going to be fun and funky, aimed at the young and fashionably young at heart, you'd be wasting your time and investment by adding in a few 9ct dainty ruby stud earrings. Worse, you'd be diluting your image, confusing potential customers and alienating both sets. Think back to your market research. If a store mixed up bright fun throwaway fashion T-shirts with sensible expensive shoes, they would put off both potential customer groups.

The fun and fashionable would see the sensible shoes and be put off. The more mature ladies looking for sensible shoes, would see the funky T-shirts and also walk past!

So it's best to drop the items that lie far outside your central style. They will just confuse your image and damage the overall look of your stand.

If you decide that you will concentrate on genuine gemstone beads set with sterling silver, drop the jewellery you've made with plated parts and bright acrylic beads.

Focus on creating a whole collection of designs that will look like they come from the same designer rather than having a mix and not match approach that will end up looking home-made rather than handmade.

Who is your target customer

The best way of creating this collection is the way that big marketing companies go about it.

Decide who is your target customer is and design for her.

You build up a picture of the person you think will be buying your jewellery. What sort of age might she be? Which of those fashion shops would she be buying in? Will she be keeping up with the latest trends or going for the classics? Will she be buying for her daughters as well as herself?

You don't want to be too rigid. After all you do want to sell as much jewellery as possible, but it does help focus your mind if you have a target customer to think about as you're planning.

Creating your brand

Your image doesn't finish with your jewellery design.

When you are designing and deciding on your target customer, think about how you will present your designs.

What name will you give your new collection. People love brands, and you have to decide on a name that you will put on your business cards and your leaflets. It can be your own name or an adaptation of your name or something completely different.

For instance, someone called Sarah Jane could call her new jewellery business Sarah Jane

Jewellery, Sarah Jane Designs, SJ Jewellery, SJ Silver Jewellery. She could pick something entirely different. Bridal Creations, Glitz & Glamour, Gorgeous Goth Gems.

A brand name gives your customers something to follow. If they see a list of exhibitors at a craft fair, they will know whether you will be there. They'll be able to tell their friends who to look for. It's much better if they can say, look for Glitz and Glamour, rather than the tall girl with dark hair!

Designing your logo

Now that you've got this far, you have a jewellery style and a business name. You can begin to think about the image of your entire business. What will your colour scheme be? What sort of font will you use for your new business name. This is the point at which your business name becomes your logo.

Writing exactly the same word in a number of different fonts and using different colours will create different images.

Try this out on your computer. Pick a simple name and repeat it a number of times on the page. Then use a different font each time. Once you print it out, you will see what a difference it makes. Again learn from the professionals. They spend millions of pounds making slight alterations to their logos. It might seem a terrible waste of money, but the way a brand is written affects the way we see them, and how we think of their services or their products.

Bridal Creations , written in a traditional script font that is often used for bridal businesses will give the impression of being traditional and elegant. Pictures of pearl tiaras and sparkling Austrian crystal necklaces will spring to mind as soon as someone reads your name. But if you want to attract the more funky brides to your funky jewellery, then you want to choose a font and a style that will show them that you have something different to offer right from the very start. And that start comes with your logo.

Now you're really beginning to get somewhere, you know what kind of jewellery you're going to design and who you're going to sell it to. And you know what your company image looks like now that you've developed your business name and your logo. You're beginning to feel like a real business.

None of these things have to cost you a fortune or even take that long to create, but it makes the difference between selling some home-made jewellery at a church fete and selling your unique handmade designs at craft fairs and other events.

Having formed this idea of your style, you will find it easier to make other decisions about your new business. Deciding what your colour scheme is. What colour covers you will have for your table. What type of packaging you will choose, what type of promotions you will run. It will even help focus your mind so that you can decide where you will sell your handmade designs.

Unique Selling Point

Otherwise known as your USP, every business should have a unique selling point, but what is it!

It's what sets you, your business and your jewellery, apart from other people. It's what your business stands for. It's what's important to you. It is also back to the point of not trying to be everything to everyone.

Working out what your USP is can help you focus your mind on what you actually want to do and how you want to be seen.

Okay, at its simplest, you want to sell your handmade jewellery.

But why do you want to make jewellery? Is one of your aims to get away from the mass production that we see nowadays. Do you love creating something totally unique, each piece is being a part of your own personality.

Do you want each of your intricate bead work patterns to be a unique work of art? Something collectable and valued as a piece of work as much as a piece of jewellery.

Do you concentrate on ethical sourcing of your gemstones, or do you focus on recycling in your design work?

Take some time about your USP. It's a worthwhile process personally as well as for your business. It means that you will be concentrating on why you have started selling your handmade jewellery. What do you love about making jewellery, what do you love about the materials that you use. What are your passions, after all this is not just a job, you have taken the decision to start a creative business of your own, and it's very exciting! If it's not exciting, it might be time to rethink things because it takes quite a lot of work, and you'll probably find yourself making jewellery late into the night sometimes, so it definitely needs to be something that you love doing. And that is the best part about this whole process, being able to make money from something you love doing. It means that you never really go to work!

Presenting Yourself

Setting out your stall

When you're selling face-to-face, whether it's at markets, country fairs, school or church events, craft fairs, wedding shows or house parties -your main display counter will be a table.

Normally a 6' x 2' table that you have to be prepared to adapt, because unless you use your own table you will be taking potluck. Some will be narrow, some wide, some hotels will even put out roundtables (although luckily not many!)

Even if you book a space at a large professional exhibition, you will still normally start with a table inside your booth. You can move on to a display of shelves and glass cabinets if you are going to be concentrating your business on exhibition space, but you won't begin your career with that type of investment.

So - a 6 foot table. How do you turn that into an attractive shopfront?

You need four basic things:
A cover
Height
Display stands.
Lighting

The cover.

The cover is quite straightforward. It wants to be big enough to cover your table to the floor. It looks very amateurish to have it hanging in midair. You want to create your own space, and while the top of the table is your selling space, under the table is your store room and you don't want to leave the store room wide open for the public to see!

You can use standard tablecloths or sheets if you need to but it's worth setting yourself up properly in the first place.

Find a fabric shop, preferably one that sells upholstery and curtain fabric and buy some sheeting.

Sheeting is wide enough to cover the top and front of your stand and you can buy enough length to stretch past each end of the table so that you can create a tidy corner with the aid of some hospital corners and safety pins. (For those who don't know, a hospital corner is a way of tidily folding the bedsheets!)

You will also have a choice of colours. The colour of your cloth will be the basis of your whole look and is a major part of your overall style.

Crisp white – (which needs to be kept spotlessly clean)
Elegant black or Goth Black
Rich burgundy.
Cool blue
Funky yellow
Pretty pink

Whatever colour you choose you will want the rest of your display to work with it, so it is a very important decision. Don't be tempted to grab the first thing you find and think that will do. If you don't put some thought into it at this stage you will end up replacing your covers quite quickly which is an unnecessary expense.

It's also worth buying some extra fabric so that you can use this to cover any extra boxes that you will use.

If you can't find exactly the colour you've decided on, buy white sheeting and dye it to the colour you want. If you do choose this method make sure that you prepare more fabric than you think you'll need. There will be times when you book more space at a fair and you'll need cloths for at least a 12ft display.

Height

A flat 6 x 2 table with jewellery just lying on it will look - well flat!

Boring and uninteresting. Dull.

You get the idea? It will look amateurish and apart from anything else, you're limiting your display space

Think back to that shopping centre. Did any of the jewellery shops have their jewellery lying flat on the bottom of the window display? No! They have hundreds of pounds worth of display stands layered up on beautiful shelving to show everything off.

Your version doesn't need cost hundreds of pounds, there are lots of ways that you can create the same sort of effect. Be creative.

Height adds interest, it adds variation, it adds space.

One of the easiest ways to add height is to unpack the boxes you carry everything in, turn them upside down and cover them in smaller cloths that match your main table cover.

If you do use this method, then your choice of storage box becomes a bit more important. You want to select suitable sizes, not too big and not too small, and possibly a variety of sizes. You also want to choose boxes with flat bases, so that they will create good, stable shelving.

One of the best types of box is a sturdy cardboard case that fruit and vegetables are delivered in to the greengrocers and supermarkets. They are strong, often have good handle slots for carrying, they stack on top of one another, they have flat bases and they're free!

Once you drape your cloth over them, no one will guess how humble your beautiful shelving really is.

Display stands

Now that you have the main bones of your counter, you can add even more height.

The type of height you will need depends on the type of jewellery you've made.

If you have lots of earrings or pendants on cords, you might want to create some tall, frame like displays that can take a number of pendants or pairs of earrings. You can buy this type of display from professional jewellery packaging companies, or if you're creative (which you are) you can make some from photo frames or cork boards, or even some mount board from your local Art shop.

Other styles of jewellery require other types of display. After all, you will need some way of displaying your individual star pieces of jewellery.

You will see some people selling jewellery all just laid out flat on a flat table. But this makes nothing of the individual pieces and it tends to looks amateurish. It does have its place, for instance if you want to give the impression of selling very low value pieces. And I say the impression because these aren't often sold at a low price, they are just perceived as cheap. But sometimes they actually cost more money than genuine gemstone and sterling silver pieces. This style of display, if it's done deliberately, is done to create the image of pile it high, sell it cheap and can work well in a flea market or car boot sale or even a school table top sale where you want to create the impression of affordability.

But in most cases you will want to create a better image for your handcrafted work. Whatever materials you work with, you have put time and skill into the piece and you want to show it off at its best.

If you make necklaces or large pendants, you probably want to use some jewellery busts. If you make bracelets you may want a stand that you can drape a number of bracelets on.

There are many types of jewellery stand, as you can see when you look at a jewellery shop window, and while you don't need them all you probably need a selection.

Most bead suppliers also sell display material and you can also find some on the Internet, while some designs can be unique and made with your computer and some good quality card.

Lighting

It's very tempting to ignore lighting, especially when you are first starting out, but that is a mistake.

Think of the way jewellery glitters in jewellery shop windows. It's not just that they're diamonds, gemstones and precious metals, they are very well lit!

And when you look at other stands around you at your first craft show, you will notice that those crafters who know what they are doing - have lights!

When you are deciding on your lights, there are certain things to take into account. They need to be sturdy and easy to carry around. Take the weight into account as well, you will have to carry them from fair to fair and at times, you will have to carry them upstairs or the length of long marquees.

Look around at various shops for your lights. You don't need to go for special - and normally expensive - professional shop display lighting. Nowadays, you can find plenty of choice in home decor or office supply stores.

The style of lighting will depend on your overall display. If you have a large sturdy framework, you can clip lights to that. If your display is more open, you probably need freestanding lights.

The right lighting will really make your stand and your beautiful, handmade jewellery stand out. And remember, the first part of making a sale is getting a customer's attention in the first place.

You will also need to have extension cables in your equipment pack, as you will often have to connect to the power supply at a distance.

Many organisers will require that you have your electrical equipment tested. A PAT certificate (portable appliance testing) is required for each piece of equipment and lasts 12 months.

There are all sorts of other things, you can add to your stand to attract attention and what you choose will depend on your style. You could decide to display one of your main pieces on a jewellery bust on a Lazy Susan so that it catches the light as it turns, or you could use a digital photo frame to showcase some of your other designs. Make sure that you have a mirror on your stand whether it is part of your display or simply available to hand to your customer.

Exhibition Banners

However you design your table, the first task of your stand is to be noticed.

You may well be in hall with 50, 70 or over 100 other craft stalls, so you want people to notice yours. You want them to stop, look at your jewellery and of course you want them to buy. But if you don't attract them in the first place none of that can happen.

The exhibition banner displayed behind your table is a great way of doing this. It's an advert that people can see from a distance. You can include pictures of your jewellery on the banner so that they have an idea of what you have on offer before they risk becoming too close!

Many of the copy and print centres and some of the big stationery stores now produce this kind of banner or stand for you from about £50. So if you're planning on doing a number of events this can be a very good investment. Do think of the design carefully. If you use a banner this will be your largest visual advert, so you want to make sure that it is sending the message you want and that it is giving people the correct idea about your style.

The rest of your equipment bag

There are other things that you need to make sure you have with you when you set out to do a show.

A cash float. Yes, I know the plan is to take money, but you also need to have some with you in the first place. Most people get their money from cash machines nowadays, so they will be presenting you with beautifully crisp £10 and £20 notes, you will need to have some change for them if you want to make a sale. Make sure you have a good selection of £5 notes, £1 coins, silver and copper if you're going to set your prices at £4.99, £9.99, £14.99 etc.

You also want to keep your cash safe. So you will need a cash box to make it easy to sort out your coins, and a bag that you can keep attached to you to keep all the hundreds of £10 notes safe.

You'll need a calculator to add up all the sales, a note book to keep a record of them and also to take notes for special orders that you will be sending out, so of course you'll need a pen!

Depending on how you have decided to display your jewellery, you might need a supply of price labels, some paper bags or gift bags and tissue paper for packaging, or you might need a supply of the jewellery boxes that you will be using so that you can keep topping up your display as you make sales.

If you're working on your own, you'll need to take some food and drink with you as you might not be able to leave your stall. Once you get used to the fairs you are doing you will know if food is available easily or if you can ask your neighbour to watch things for you. Some organisers don't allow you to eat at your stand – and I wouldn't recommend sitting down to a large meal at any event, but a sandwich and a bottle of water can keep you going through a long day.

Packaging your product

Obviously, when a customer buys a piece of jewellery from you it has to be packaged in some way. But what way?

Creating an image

In the jewellery world image is vital, as we been discovering. Some brands are actually identified by their packaging as much as by their jewellery. Think of the duck egg blue box tied with a white satin ribbon. Since they were designed in 1837, the Tiffany blue box can be as important as the jewellery inside it when someone is deciding to make a purchase.

Packaging isn't simply to protect the purchase. After all, you could just put the bracelet that the client has purchased in a clear plastic bag. I've even seen some crafters wrap their work in old newspapers (not jewellers I have to add!) and while that might save some money it certainly doesn't create much of an impression.

A piece of jewellery is never an absolute necessity. It's a treat, a little personal luxury and it should feel that way. So it's very important to put some thought and investment into your packaging. After all, it is all part of your product and you should price it into your cost in the same way as you do the beads and the findings you use in a piece.

Jewellery is a strange product in some ways.

The value isn't really down to the actual materials but the perceived value of the piece, which is all to do with the standard of your workmanship, the amount of work in the design, the way you present it, where it's sold and how it is packaged.

We will assume that, seeing as you are reading this book, the standard of your workmanship has already reached a level that customers will be happy with.

The amount of work in a design can be a little bit more difficult to value. Obviously a very intricate piece of work will require a higher price. But there are some big brands, who can charge big prices but actually produce very basic designs. Well made but very basic!

Most people are not very good at judging the actual value of jewellery, so the way you present and package it will create a pricing level.

A pair of Amethyst earrings on a plastic card will give the image of a chain store or supermarket. The same pair in a luxurious jewellery box will appear much more valuable. So even though the box will probably cost you more than the parts for the earrings, it would be a good investment if you are selling in the kind of market place where you can pitch your jewellery at that level.

There are many ways of packaging between these two styles and this is an important decision, as it will set the style and image of your stand, indeed of your collection and your business as a whole.

So what can you choose and what image doesn't create?

Plastic or card tab tops

This is the type of style often associated with fashion jewellery that is found in supermarkets, fashion stores or market stalls. This tends to make your jewellery look mass produced rather than handmade. It also creates the image of throwaway jewellery, you need a new necklace to go with the outfit you're wearing tonight. Rather than choosing a piece that you will wear for years and pass on to your family.

An alternative version to the basic tab top, is to use your own personalised handmade tag attached to your jewellery or in the case of earrings, your jewellery attached to it. This gives a completely different image, creating the feeling of unique handmade pieces only available from you, which of course they are.

You can create your own tags on a computer with some basic design software. They work as an introduction to your jewellery brand. The front will normally have your name and logo, while the back of the tag will give some contact information such as your phone number or website address. You should include something with every sale that gives your contact details to your customer.

Organza bags and velvet pouches

The organza bag tends to create the image of

something modern and trendy, especially with semiprecious gems such as bead bracelets and bead necklaces, while velvet bags are more traditionally used for a string of pearls and these give your jewellery and more traditional, richer image. The benefits of using pouches are that they are less expensive than jewellery boxes and they are easier to pack. If you use boxes as your packaging you'll find yourself carrying quite a lot of bulk, as opposed to using organza bags or velvet pouches. They are also more environmentally friendly, jewellery boxes have quite a lot of parts to them and are very often thrown away, while a pouch is simple fabric and will probably be used to keep the jewellery in or reused for something else.

If you intend to post your jewellery they will also reduce the cost of your postage considerably, because the Royal Mail now bases their charges on the size of the package and most jewellery boxes will fall into the size of small package rather than large letter and there is a significant difference in the price of postage.

Jewellery boxes.

Jewellery boxes come in a huge range of designs from the basic cardboard box to the exclusive polished wooden box.

The basic cardboard box with cotton filled liner comes in many sizes and colours to suit different types of jewellery from small earrings to large bead necklaces. These boxes are traditionally used with handmade bead jewellery, as they are reasonably priced, but they still add an extra dimension to your jewellery. Many people wanting to buy a your work as a gift will expect it to be boxed. However the fibrous cotton lining, which is perfect for bead jewellery can get caught on more delicate pieces.

Higher end cardboard and plastic boxes have more solid foam inserts which are suitable for more delicate jewellery.

From there, the choice is almost endless. Flocked boxes, luxurious leatherette boxes, high quality wooden boxes and even the novelty boxes that are particularly popular at Christmas, although these are mostly designed for rings and small earrings.

If you specialise in certain style of jewellery for instance, wedding jewellery, you might decide to package it in a more high end jewellery box which will emphasise the image of it being an heirloom piece.

You can choose the colour of your box to match the rest of your style, creating a corporate image and you can have them printed with your logo to create a stronger image of your brand. Again, this can sound as if it's only for the big boys, but the whole idea of a corporate image is simply that everything works together. So if you have chosen burgundy as the basic colour of your range, using a burgundy table covering, burgundy print on your tags and burgundy in your logo, it make sense to continue that and use burgundy jewellery boxes.

Packaging the packaging

Your packaging and presentation doesn't stop with the jewellery box or pouch.

Think about how you are going to hand it over. After all, you not just going to hand somebody a jewellery box. You will want to put it in an outer bag, possibly a small gift bag, and you must always include some form of business card. It could be a simple business card with your name or business name, your logo and contact details. Or it could be a special romance card giving some information about you, how you design your jewellery, what your inspiration is, or details about the specific piece of jewellery and gemstones you have used.

I had a friend at craft shows who put all her items in little boxes. The boxes were very nice, but the finishing touch was the fact that she tied them all with beautiful ribbon. It took a little bit of extra time, and it made every customer feel that she was putting a little bit of extra effort into their purchase. People didn't mid waiting, they didn't even mind waiting while she finished packing someone else's order. She had lots of repeat customers!

And of course the packaging can be an advert in itself. If you put your jewellery into a lovely little gift bag, which just so happens to have your logo hanging on a tag from the bag handle, then every one of your customers will be advertising you as they walk around the rest of the event. Just another little marketing idea you can liberate from the large stores and designer companies!

Choose your packaging to suit your image. There's a huge range of packaging available. You might choose natural jute or hemp bags to suit your jewellery if you work with the natural wooden beads or recycled charms.

Small brown paper bags might be exactly the kind of look you want if you create jewellery out of natural materials.

If you use silver clay to record a babies footprint in a unique silver pendant, then you could use pale pink and blues and other pastel colours in your packaging.

Glamorous jewellery might call for elegant black and gold bags, while delicate silver jewellery might look perfect in silver hologram gift bags.

You could even buy plain craft bags and design the whole look yourself, even having a rubberstamp made of your logo and printing the bags yourself.

Pricing your jewellery

Pricing your jewellery can be one of the most difficult parts of setting up your own business.

Most people undervalue themselves and feel nervous at first about the idea of asking people to pay for the jewellery they have made. But after all, if you are reading this book you have taken the decision to sell your handmade jewellery, and therefore you should expect to be paid for it. It is no longer a hobby and you shouldn't treat it as one. This is now a business

As I mentioned earlier in the book, jewellery can be an odd product to price. It is more than the sum of its parts, in fact exactly the same parts can be made into very similar pieces of jewellery but priced a completely different levels depending upon where they are sold and how they are packaged.

It's one of those products, where your pricing is as much to do with what the market will stand as the actual costs of the materials.

Your reputation as a designer will also affect how much you can charge, so you will find that as time goes on you can price the same pieces at a higher level. Just ease the prices up gently as you do more shows.

And of course your presentation is a vital part of your pricing. As long as the quality of your work is good, if you present it as an exclusive piece then it will be viewed as more valuable.

Work out the cost of each piece

One of the biggest problems people have when starting out selling jewellery is not to overprice it, but to underprice it.

They undervalue their work and potential customers see the price on the tag rather than what the gems, beads or metals that the piece actually contains and they will judge it as cheap jewellery even if you have used sterling silver and genuine gemstones.

So there are various stages to pricing for jewellery.

First of all, you obviously have to know the actual costs of your jewellery. Itemise each piece you have used in your design. How much cord, how many headpins, how much wire or elastic, how many spacer beads and of course how many actual beads.

When you buy a strand of beads, count how many actual beads you get on the strand so that you know how much each individual bead costs you.

Also remember to include the cost of actually getting the stock, for instance the cost of the journey to the warehouse or the delivery charge for the package if you're buying your parts by mail-order or through the Internet. Divide the cost by the amount of beads or findings you have purchased and add that amount to the price of each item.

For instance, if the delivery is £5.00 and you have bought 10 strands of beads at £7.00 each, then each strand actually cost you £7.50.

Another thing to remember is to add the VAT onto your individual price.

It can be far too easy to forget these extras when you're first working out your costs. When you place an order for a number of items, you're perfectly well aware of the total amount you have spent, but when it comes to working out the price of each individual strand or bead, it can be far too easy to look at the price label on the strand and forget everything else.

So when you start, take the time to work out these costs for each individual design you make.

When you make a design using wire, measure how much actual wire you have used and work out how much it cost you.

How much did you pay for the ear hooks, the head pins and eye pins, how much was each 3mm sterling silver bead and how many did you use.

Once you have an accurate price for the components of your design you also need to take into account how long it took to make it, how much the packaging is going to cost, and how much it is going to cost you to sell it. For instance the commission you pay or how much rent you will pay for your stall must be added to your items. After all you have to pay it.

Another mistake that many new jewellers make is to fail to take into account the cost of their labour, especially when they are expanding a hobby.

While there's doubt that it is definitely a joy to be paid to do what you love doing, the important part there is 'to be paid'. It might be all right to do your first couple of fairs for the love of it, you must remember that you are investing your time in making the jewellery, getting all the parts, finding packaging and display material and the time you actually spend at the fair, and that time could be invested elsewhere. So you must include the labour costs in your calculation.

Time yourself when you are making a pair of earrings, a bracelet or a necklace. Don't time the first piece that you make in that design because you will get faster once you've learnt a technique. Once you know the piece takes on average 10 minutes or 20 minutes or 2 hours, you can decide how much you want to be paid for that time.

Your jewellery making may also incur other costs, such as electricity, wear and tear on a piece of domestic equipment such as an oven if you make your own silver clay components. Don't forget these costs, they might not be much when you are making a few pieces for yourself but they will begin to add up once you start producing enough for your business and the bills will have to be paid.

The final part of the equation is profit.

Profit isn't a dirty word. Every business, no matter how large or small needs to make a profit if it is to have a future. Even a charity has to make its own form of profit otherwise, after all the costs are paid it has nothing to give to the charity.

The level of profit that you want is entirely up to you, but don't set it too low.

Your wholesale price

Once you've been through all the stages, and you've come up with the cost of producing your jewellery, you have the price that you must sell it at to avoid losing money. You could call this your wholesale price, the lowest price at which you can sell your jewellery.

It is a vital price to have even if you have no intention of wholesaling, although you may want to consider it if approached by a craft shop or gallery. But there will be times when you want to offer a discount on your prices, even if it isn't for wholesale.

You might want to give a discount to regular customers. You will need to give a discount to party organisers if you do party plan. You might want to run a promotion involving a discount or many other types of offer. Your general price must be set so that it allows you to discount, and you can't discount below your cost price – there's no point in losing money on each sale you make!

So decide what your absolute minimum price is and then you will know how much you can afford to sell it for.

Setting the price of your product

Now you know how much it actually costs you

to produce a pair of earrings but that's only the first stage of deciding what you will actually sell them for.

As I said, don't be tempted to simply cover your costs and add a little bit of profit. If your jewellery is priced too cheaply it will be considered cheap.

At this stage you have to decide where you want to pitch your product. Who do you want to sell it to? Who do you have the opportunity of selling it to? At one end of the scale there is no point in selling your high quality unique designer pieces too cheaply because your potential customer will not see the value they'll just see the price and you'll damage the number of sales.

But at the other end of the scale, there are times when you will want your jewellery to appear inexpensive, for instance if you're selling small stretchy bracelets for children at a school fair or inexpensive pairs of earrings as pocket money gifts.

Although the biggest danger for new jewellers, indeed new crafters in general, is to underprice their product, you also want to avoid overpricing it.

I also find that it's a good idea to have plenty of choice under £10 level. In fact at some fairs, under the £5 level. Although I will have exclusive pieces in the £75-£100 plus range, and it's very nice when they sell, the main turnover comes from impulse buys. Unless you're selling at very exclusive fairs, it's unusual to sell many individual items are over £100. That is the kind of fair and the kind of level you want to work up to, rather than the point that you start your career at.

In general, jewellery is one of those products when the pricing comes down to what the market will stand. It can sound very imprecise and really quite unfair, but it is the fact.

Someone who has developed a name as a designer and is selling through a store or website or at a craft event that backs up the image of expensive designer pieces, can demand a much higher price for their jewellery, even fairly basic designs. If you look around, you will be able to find sterling silver, shepherds hook earrings featuring simple 8mm gemstone beads being sold at £70 or £80 a pair. You will also find some craft makers selling them at £.99 a pair. It will be very nice, but wishful thinking most of the time, to think that we could target the £70 a pair - but I hope you would never consider selling for £.99!

The exact price that you decide on is up to you. Look around at your competitors to get an idea of the prices in your market area, but don't be tempted to simply undercut the lowest price.

In any market, selling anything, you will always find somebody who is willing to charge less. Their entire marketing plan centres around being cheaper than anyone else, but unless you can produce millions of items in China, and you can afford to lose enough money to undercut your competitors until they go bankrupt, there is absolutely no future in this business model. No matter how low you set your prices, somebody will come along and undercut you. Remember, it is perfectly possible to turn over millions of pounds and lose money, look at the banks! Profit is what will pay the bills when they come in and will allow you to invest in new beads and findings and book more fairs and events.

So do get a feel for the prices that others are charging for jewellery that is similar to yours. Compare that to how much your costs are and find a price that you are comfortable with.

One of the great things about selling direct to your customer is that you can change your prices quickly if you feel is necessary although you don't want to do this too often. For instance, you don't want to make a habit of selling a pair of earrings at £15 one week and then £10 in the next week, because you will upset your regular customers. But you can alter your prices up or down, and adjust them to the way the item is selling.

You could find that necklace that takes a lot of making, sells out straight away every time and you can't keep up with that design. Wonderful of course! We all love the idea of selling out! But you might still be able to sell as many as you can make if you put the price up. After all, if it doesn't work, you can always reduce it again or even put it on special offer!

How to Promote yourself

Promoting your new jewellery business can take a number of different forms.

The Oxford English dictionary defines 'promotion' as an activity that supports or encourages a venture and the publicising of a product or venture, so as to increase sales or public awareness.

Many people think of a promotion as being simply discounting prices, and while that is a valid method of attracting more customers, promoting your business can and should take many more forms than simply relying on price.

Price promotions

We are surrounded by promotions in the retail world.

BOGOF's
50% discount.
Three-for-two
even 70% off!
January sale.
Christmas event

They can all sound very tempting, and some of them even work, attracting us to buy things we didn't really want and certainly didn't intend to buy. But we have become quite jaded as consumers, simply not believing most of these promises. The half price sale finishes on Sunday and 50% off sale starts on Monday!

But that doesn't mean that you should

completely forget about developing your own promotions and special offers, you just have to be a bit more imaginative with them.

Bundled discounts

This is the type of marketing policy that covers things like the BOGOF that you find at supermarkets, but it doesn't have to be that obvious. Clearly, if you're going to offer Buy One Get One Free, the price of each one has to cover the costs of two.

You might decide that your marketing policy is to offer bargains, to be the discount outlet of the craft fair, in which case you've probably gone for bright, primary colours in your design and basic packaging. If this is your brand style you will want to make a show of your discount offers because this will be your main selling point.

But if your style is dainty gemstone jewellery or unique pieces of handmade glass made into pendants, you don't really want your elegant craft stall to look like supermarket. In this case you can still introduce the idea of bundled discounts in a more subtle way.

For instance, if you sell a necklace and a pair of earrings that match, but you normally sell them separately, you can have a discount for buying the set.

If you sell bracelet charms, you could have an offer where a customer who purchases four charms, receives a fifth one free.

If you sell pendants and silver chains separately

you could have a discount price for the chain when it is purchased with a pendant.

Time specific discounts.

You could have a 'special show price' on a particular type of item. You can set a discount 'just for this event.'

You see this kind of promotion quite regularly at large events, Normally offered by the large, professional companies that travel the country selling at flower shows, County shows, horse shows and the like. If you buy from them on the day, you pay a special show price. If you purchase later from their website, the item will cost you more.

The whole idea of this is to make people part with their money there and then, rather than picking up a leaflet, going away and thinking about it. It's a style of promotion that is quite often used for more expensive products, where people are more likely to go away and think about it rather than making an impulse purchase, but it can work on any type of product. The idea is to make people buy it now.

Free gifts

Everyone loves something free.

Free is a magic word in marketing.

Free will stop almost anyone in their tracks and make them look.

So how can you use this marketing idea in your business.

Some people literally give something away free, for instance, they have a bowl of boiled sweets on the counter with the idea that this will make people stop and take a sweet. Of course they will stop and take a sweet and some of them might even look at your jewellery while doing it!

I prefer to make people work for their free gift or more to the point, buy something.

The best way of using the free gift marketing method is to encourage people to buy more. Spend over £20 and receive a free jewelled hair clip. Spend over £50 and receive a free pair of earrings. Spend over £10 and receive a free gift box. The exact details, the exact levels of spend, and the free gift is entirely up to you. It will depend on your style. It will depend on the type of customer you're aiming at, and it will depend on your profit margins.

Sale time

The problem with the word Sale is that it has been overused and has lost its power to attract. Some shops constantly have sales and people stop looking.

But it can still be worth using. If you have some stock that just isn't selling it can be worth bundling together and putting the word sale on it. I would try various other methods first. Altering the prices, up as well as down. Sometimes an item that is not selling will suddenly become a bestseller when you put the price up!

A bargain basket can be a very good way of

selling designs that you want to reduce in price. There's something about a bargain basket box that just attracts people! They love rooting through looking for a bargain. Of course you have to make sure that your jewellery is not just going to end up in a tangled knot at the bottom of the basket. How you manage this problem will depend on the designs you use in the first place. If you already package your jewellery, then it should be safe enough in a basket. But if you normally have your bead necklaces laid out on the counter you might want to put each of them in a plastic bag first.

Product promotion.

Although price promotions are fine to use at one time or another, you should have promotions that are a continual part of your business plan.

You should promote your business.

These type of promotions are to encourage customer loyalty, create the style of your brand, remind potential customers about you, and of course to increase sales.

Make sure that everyone who has a piece of your jewellery, knows that it is your jewellery. Some events, especially charity events, ask you to provide a gift for their raffle. And of course you want to support the charity, but make sure that whoever wins your piece of jewellery knows where it's from. There's nothing wrong with supporting your business as well as the charity.

When a customer buys a piece of your jewellery, make sure that they have the details of where they can find you and how they can contact you so that they can make future purchases. When someone receives some of your jewellery as a gift, make sure they know that you are the designer and how they can purchase more pieces.

Every piece of jewellery that leaves your stall should be branded in some way. The way you add your logo will depend on the style of your jewellery but don't think that it has to be something expensively produced by a professional printer. The beauty of your jewellery is that it is individually handmade, so there's nothing wrong with the packaging being handmade as well. In fact it adds to your overall style.

If you make a chunky vintage style jewellery, why not find some manila luggage tags and write your details by hand on them. If your jewellery is very delicate, create a delicate leaflet to put in the box with it.

Talking about your jewellery.

One of the nice things about selling face-to-face is the fact that you actually get a chance to meet your customers. So make the most of it.

They could buy a piece of jewellery anywhere. At any of the other stalls at the fair, at any fashion shop, jewellery shop or even supermarket. But they want to buy the jewellery from you. So talk to them about it.

When you look around at many events, you will always find some designers who just sit behind their stall, often reading a book. Put yourself in the position of the potential customer. If you were thinking of buying something from that stall, you'd probably just walk past. Why should you show interest in their work if they can't show interest in you. You also have to remember that a lot of people would feel uncomfortable about disturbing someone who has obviously got something better to do than to talk to them.

So, stand behind or to the side of your stall. Smile at people, engage with them, say hello. You don't have to pounce on every potential customer, that is counter-productive. But you should show them that you are aware that they are there and that you are willing to talk to them if they would like.

When you do open a conversation, talk about your jewellery. What makes it different? What is your USP (unique selling point). After all, you now know what your style is, so you should also know why your jewellery is different to anyone else's.

Do you always include a piece of Jade in your design, because it is the gem of health, wealth and long life?

Are your designs made from pieces of polished glass that you personally collect from the beach?

Is recycling an important aspect of your design?

What led you into designing handmade jewellery, what is your story?

Tell them that you can customise pieces, changing the type of ear fastening, altering the length of a bracelet or making a certain design in different colours. Taking orders for bespoke jewellery can be a very valuable addition to your new business.

When somebody does buy a necklace, point out - without pressure - that you do earrings to match.

And don't be afraid to talk to someone, even though you have a very good feeling that they are not going to buy anything from you, at least today. They may well come back on another day when they do want to buy a piece of jewellery, and they will remember that you were friendly and didn't pressurise them. Or you might sell to the people who were listening to your conversation - lots of people prefer to join a crowd when they wouldn't approach you themselves.

Demonstrating your craft.

This might sound a bit odd, showing other people how to compete with you! But in fact, showing people how to do a craft can be a very good way of selling to them.

It can work in two different ways. You can create starter packs, so that you can teach people how to create their own jewellery. Next time you're at a large craft shop, look around at how many products are being sold to crafters. There's nothing to stop you put in your own product range together and selling these starter packs to your students.

You should also have some of your own handmade designs with you when you demonstrate. People who are interested in learning how to make jewellery are interested in jewellery. And while they will enjoy making their own. They are beginners, and your designs will be much more professional. So don't be surprised when you sell some of the samples you've taken with you. In fact, that should be part of your plan! Also make sure that you take plenty of promotional literature. You want them to be able to find you when they decide they want to buy a piece of handmade jewellery.

You can do these demonstrations to a number of different groups. Some libraries have regular events for people to learn new skills. You might find that you can work with the girl guides or brownies or as entertainment at birthday parties. You could offer your skills to women's groups or maybe even set up a package and offer it for hen parties. Learn to think outside the box.

Seasonal promotions

There are certain times of the year that are just made for jewellery and especially jewellery gifts.

The main ones of course, are Christmas and Valentine's Day and don't forget Mother's Day, and Father's Day if you make men's jewellery.

There are also some other dates that you might want to add to your list. Halloween is getting more and more popular, and there are plenty of people who love to dress up for Halloween and would certainly buy some jewellery if it fitted in with their costume. Depending on your style, you can really go to town on some over the top Halloween designs.

You might also be able to create designs as Easter presents and for first Communions and confirmations. If your design style lends itself to delicate crosses, these celebrations would be perfect for you. You could even think about creating some very special rosary beads.

And of course don't forget the end of the school year. This can give you two separate opportunities, gifts for teachers and graduation gifts.

Which of these events you decide to use for your promotions will depend on the type of jewellery that you design, and how and where you sell it. You will probably be able to think of some more events that would be perfect for your brand.

The Christmas season

The Christmas season is arguably the most important part of the year for your new jewellery business.

It's that time of the year when you will find the most events, and some of the biggest events. The season runs from early October to about the middle of December. The main out-of-town Christmas fairs are completed by the end of November or the very beginning of December and then events such as Christmas markets will run almost up to the holiday itself.

Some crafters spend most of the year preparing for the Christmas season, and for any crafter it can be the most hectic time of the year - in fact, it's best if you get your own Christmas family preparations done before October!

As a jewellery maker this is an ideal season. Jewellery is such an easy gift to give and it can cover the whole range of gift giving. In fact, you can expand your range by offering cuff links, tie pins, key rings, bookmarks or letter openers.

Your customers can find the perfect gift for almost anybody and it will be unique. Whoever they give it to won't be able to go to the January sales and see how much they spent! And they don't have to worry about someone else giving exactly the same gift - a problem you do have to consider when you choose a book or DVD!

All styles of jewellery can be adapted for the Christmas gift market.

If you focus on fashion jewellery and fun and funky designs then Christmas tree bauble earrings and bright red and green bangles might be the way you decide to go. On the other hand, you may prefer to simply make more of your normal designs and package them beautifully so that they are a gift that somebody can simply purchase and give, already boxed and ready to be presented, especially if you add a little gift bag.

The seasonal promotion doesn't just have to stop with your actually jewellery and how you package it.

You can – and should - carry the idea through to your entire shopfront.

Again, take a leaf out of all the experts book. The department stores spend thousands of pounds decorating their windows. The shopping centres make a big feature of their Christmas decorations, and town centres make an entire event out of turning on the Christmas lights. They do this because it attracts customers, and it puts them in the Christmas mood, which makes them think of buying presents and spending money.

So join in. Decorate your table. Use tinsel or fairy lights along the front. Maybe you have enough room for a miniature Christmas tree.

Whatever you decide, make your stall festive, encourage people to think of buying Christmas gifts when they see your display.

If you have decided to use beautiful gift boxes as part of your promotion, display them on your table.

Think how the stores display all the beautiful gift wrapped boxes that they have on offer at this time of the year. Very often the products inside them are nothing special. Body lotions, shower gels, hand creams, maybe a china mug with some sweets inside it , maybe a tie and some cufflinks. Many of these gifts contain quite ordinary products but they are packaged in a beautiful way in beautiful boxes with ribbon around them. It's easy to just buy them, take them home and put them under the tree.

People are always short of time, especially at Christmas time, and buying these types of ready to give gifts is so much to do, it takes the thinking and the work out of the process. So they are attracted to anything that will save them time and make life easy. Yes, it would be cheaper to buy a nice box and all the body lotions and package them yourself, but people don't do that, they pay extra to have it done.

So when they see your jewellery, beautifully packaged and presented it will automatically look more like a gift. And that's the effect you want.

This might also be a time to use one of the price promotions. Again, very often used by stores. The most popular one is 3 for 2 - of course remember that it's always the lowest priced item that is free!

This is another time you should learn from the experts. They have found that, particularly at Christmas, this promotion will encourage people to buy two items, rather than just one. In fact, you can find yourself spending longer in front of the shelves wondering who you will give the extra two gifts to and what you should choose, when it would be much quicker and cheaper to just pick the one you wanted in the first place. But that's the point. It works. So if the big stores can make the most of it - so can you.

Of course, do remember that they are all priced to cover the cost of the three items, even though as a shopper you feel that you are getting a bargain, and there's that wonderful magic word again – FREE!

So if you decide to use this promotion, do make sure that you work out your prices correctly. You're not actually in the business of giving away jewellery – even at Christmas!

When you're selling at the Christmas season it's all about getting the sales.

People want to buy gifts.

They will part with their money.

They have to go home with all the presents they need.

The stocking fillers. Small gifts for friends and neighbours. The gifts for teachers. They will spend their money somewhere, and your main aim at this time of the year is to get them to spend it with you. That is why you invest money in taking a stand at the fair in the first place.

Growing your business.

Where will you go from here

The decisions you make about the way you want your business to go and how you want it to grow are entirely personal.

They will depend on you, your personal circumstances, what you want to put into your business and what you want to get out of it. There is no right or wrong.

I have been in business since the late 1970s (oh, that makes me feel old. I started very young!) And for many years I ran a business with lots of staff, dealing with big multinational companies, and lots of overseas interests, and I loved it.

But things changed when I was diagnosed with M.E. (chronic fatigue syndrome). I had to make some rather drastic changes in my life. Now, I design and make healing crystal jewellery. I mentor small businesses, and give talks to start up groups. I write books on business and alternative therapies, and I run my small family business through craft fairs and events and online websites. I can work from home and set my own timetable, and I love this as well.

When you start your own business, the whole idea is to have more control over your life.

If you are starting your handmade jewellery business as you leave college or university, you will probably have great plans for creating a brand that you will be able to launch into the mainstream, and that is great. People with great brands that grow from small seeds are the lifeblood of the economy, that is how the great brands start. After all, Marks and Spencer started as a market stall in Leeds

If this is your plan, the process of selling face-to-face to your customer will allow you to develop your style. You will be able to get feedback about your jewellery and find out what people really like about it. And this will help you when you want to expand your business.

But there is nothing wrong with keeping your jewellery business small and under your own control. There are thousands of people who are making a comfortable living by designing and making jewellery that they sell face-to-face to their customers. They have a loyal following and a regular season of events that they do year after year and they have no desire to start employing people and having their own business premises.

And you will find jewellery makers that fall into the middle. They do have their own premises, maybe a workshop or a retail outlet and a small staff that help them run the business. There are no rules, you just need to find a way that suits you and your lifestyle.

Selling online.

Having a presence online can complement selling face-to-face.

When you are talking to people at a craft event you can direct them to your website or some of your other designs on etsy or eBay.

You can use your blog to keep in contact with your regular customers, or create an e-mail list so that you can keep your customers up to date and let them know about the latest craft events.

If you do party plan you can have a website that you can direct potential customers to, where they can either see your range of jewellery or they can make bookings for a party. You could even add a shop so that they can actually purchase from you on-line.

Social media is a wonderful way of keeping in contact with your customers and promoting your business. It gives the small business a voice.

The type of online presence that you choose will again depend on the style of your business, the type of jewellery that you create and who your target customer is.

If your style is fun and funky jewellery, then social media is probably perfect for you. If you specialise in wedding jewellery, your target customers will be young women, and again social media is a perfect way of connecting with them and keeping in contact. In fact, wedding jewellery is one of the areas where you definitely should collect e-mail addresses. When you have someone's wedding date, you can target some promotions to those potential customers at the right time. After all, you don't just have to think about the bridal jewellery. There's jewellery for the bridesmaids, cuff links or tiepins for the groom the best man and the ushers. Wedding favours, gifts for the Mother of the Bride and the Mother of the Groom.

And of course, do remember that weddings can be a bit like party plan. Orders often lead to more orders as the bridesmaids or guests plan their own weddings. A presence on the web can be invaluable for this type of business.

The future

Once you've developed your style and have learnt what your customer wants you should have created a healthy and successful business with your handmade jewellery which will allow you to spend your time doing what you love.

The future direction of your business is entirely up to you, but you should never sit back and think you know it all!

Keep developing your style, keep adapting to changing fashions or trends. Keep your range and image fresh and relevant, it's far too easy to get complacent and stagnate, wondering why people aren't buying from you in the same way anymore. You might need to find new venues with new customers, you might need to freshen your display or introduce new designs. You need to be able to stand back and see how other people see your jewellery and your display.

And change is fun!

Part of the joy of creating your own jewellery is learning new skills, working with new products and producing new designs.

So I wish you many years of exciting jewellery designing.

A final word

The Business of Business

This book is all about marketing and selling your handmade jewellery, it is not about the legal, financial and tax requirements of running a business – any business of any size.

Find some expert advice

There are many books and courses and websites available where you can find out about these other areas of running your business and I recommend that you invest some time and money in this information so that you can avoid any pitfalls and problems in the future.

Printed in Great Britain
by Amazon.co.uk, Ltd.,
Marston Gate.